Cool Hotels

2nd edition

teNeues

Editor: Ana García Cañizares

Layout & Pre-press: Luis F. Sierra

Translations: Enrique Góngora (Spanish), Tanja Fontane (German),
Michel Ficerai (French), Maurizio Siliato (Italian)

Produced by Loft Publications
www.loftpublications.com

Published by teNeues Publishing Group

teNeues Book Division
Kaistraße 18,
40221 Düsseldorf, Germany
Tel.: 0049-(0)211-994597-0
Fax: 0049-(0)211-994597-40
E-mail: books@teneues.de

Press department:
arehn@teneues.de
Phone: 0049-2152-916-202

www.teneues.com

teNeues Publishing Company
16 West 22nd Street
New York, NY 10010, USA
Tel.: 001-212-627-9090
Fax: 001-212-627-9511

teNeues Publishing UK Ltd.
P.O. Box 402
West Byfleet, KT14 7ZF
Great Britain
Tel.: 0044-1932-403509
Fax: 0044-1932-403514

teNeues France S.A.R.L.
4, rue de Valence
75005 Paris, France
Tel.: 0033-1-55 76 62 05
Fax: 0033-1-55 76 64 19

teNeues Ibérica S.L.
c/ Velázquez, 57 6.° izda.
28001 Madrid, Spain
Tel.: 0034-657-132133

teNeues Italia
Representative Office
Via San Vittore 36/1
20123 Milano, Italy
Tel.: 0039-0347-76 40 551

ISBN-10: 3-8327-9105-1
ISBN-13: 978-3-8327-9105-6

Bibliographic information published by Die
Deutsche Bibliothek.
Die Deutsche Bibliothek lists this publication in
the Deutsche Nationalbibliografie;
detailed bibliographic data is available in the
Internet at http://dnb.ddb.de.

Over the past years, hoteliers around the world have responded even more boldly to their guests' demands for comfort, luxury and aesthetic sophistication. New trends in hotel design increasingly blur the distinction between lodging, lifestyle and living theater, creating original spaces that offer much more to visitors than just a roof over their head. The buildings that contain them can be old or new; while some hotels are built from scratch, others are crafted from previously inhabited aristocratic villas or born from old factories that have been restored to maintain their industrial aesthetic. Rather than simply providing accommodation, hotels today offer sensations and experiences catered to all kinds of travelers, from those looking for a casual but stylish loft space to others searching for a luxurious 19th century atmosphere. Location and climate have also generated specialty hotels such as ski resorts, tropical bungalows and mountains retreats in remote places which are now as cutting edge as any of the top designer hotels in major cosmopolitan centers.

Designed by international architects and a wide range of design specialists, these hotels are meticulously attentive to detail and strive for originality in every aspect. Rooms are often designed individually according to a certain theme, and the hotel programs incorporate innovative elements such as private terrace Jacuzzi's, game rooms, cooking classes, libraries and personal guides. Another key element is the constant renewal of the hotel's appearance. A continuous influx of new artwork, temporary exhibitions, updated interiors and new amenities result in spaces and services that are everything but mundane.

The most surprising hotels conceived today stand out for their ability to produce unique environments that trigger the imagination and provoke sensations, whether it be that of walking into the future, revisiting the past or entering an entirely different dimension. For many, they can also represent the idea

of the dream apartment in the city or on the countryside, providing a homely environment and a series of exceptional characteristics that they could otherwise never have the chance to experience. In addition, these hotels must be capable of matching the level of its aesthetic value to the quality and creativity of its services, offering guests not only exceptional treatment, but also features that are unconventional or out of the ordinary.

Following the successful Cool Hotels original volume edited in 2001, this second edition affords an updated review of the latest trends in hotel design with a collection of forty-nine hotels from around the world, including last year's best picks and this year's new revelations. The stunning selection of images that follows allows the reader to visit some of the most cutting-edge hotels in the world, while the uniqueness and diversity of styles, locations and venues will have the keen traveler spoiled for choice and serve as inspiration to both homeowners and designers in the field.

Seit einigen Jahren gehen Hoteliers auf der ganzen Welt immer ungewöhnlichere Wege, um den Wünschen der Gäste nach Bequemlichkeit, Luxus und Ästhetik gerecht zu werden. Neue Trends im Hotel-Design verwischen dabei die Grenzen zwischen Wohnen, Lebensstil und theatralischem Ambiente und schaffen Räume, die dem Besucher weit mehr bieten als nur ein Dach über dem Kopf. Diese Hotels befinden sich in Neubauten, traditionsreichen aristokratischen Villen oder auch in alten Fabriken, deren Industrieästhetik bei der Restaurierung bewahrt wurde. Ob Reisende ein bequemes aber gleichzeitig elegantes Loft oder das luxuriöse Ambiente des 19. Jahrhunderts suchen, diese Hotels bieten ihnen nicht allein eine Unterkunft, sondern befriedigen unterschiedlichste Bedürfnisse, indem sie ständig mit neuen Sensationen und Erlebnissen aufwarten. Spezielle Hotels, die unter Berücksichtigung klimatischer und örtlichen Gegebenheiten gebaut wurden, wie Ski-Resorts, tropische Bungalows oder Zuflüchte in den Bergen, sind inzwischen genauso avantgardistisch wie berühmte Designer-Hotels in den wichtigsten Metropolen der Welt.

Die Hotels, die dieses Buch vorstellt, wurden von international angesehenen Architekten und verschiedenen Designspezialisten gestaltet, die ihr Augenmerk insbesondere auf die Details richteten, wobei sie Originalität in allen Aspekten suchten. Die Zimmer wurden meist individuell und unter einer bestimmten Themenstellung gestaltet, während zu den Programmen der Hotels innovative Elemente wie Jacuzzis auf privaten Terrassen, Unterhaltungsräume, Kochkurse, Bibliotheken und persönliche Reiseführer gehören. Eine weitere Besonderheit, die diese Hotels kennzeichnet, ist die permanente, immer wieder überraschende Erneuerung ihres Erscheinungsbildes durch wechselnde Kunstausstellungen, die Veränderung der Inneneinrichtung und neue Service-Angebote.

Die originellsten Hotels bestechen durch ihre Fähigkeit, einmalige Umgebungen zu kreieren, die die Fantasie anregen und unvergessliche Erlebnisse hervorru-

fen, indem sie uns in die Zukunft, in die Vergangenheit oder in andere Dimensionen versetzen. Für viele Gäste stellen sie perfekte Apartments in städtischer oder ländlicher Umgebung dar, in denen man sich heimisch fühlt und die gleichzeitig Annehmlichkeiten bieten, in deren Genuss man sonst nicht kommen würde. Zudem sind die Hotels in der Lage, den hohen ästhetischen Standard mit qualitätvollem wie kreativem Service zu verbinden, der dem Gast nicht nur herausragende, sondern ebenso unkonventionelle wie außergewöhnliche Dienstleistungen bietet.

Diese zweite Auflage von Cool Hotels, das erstmals im Jahre 2001 veröffentlicht wurde, bietet einen Überblick über die neuesten Trends im Hotel-Design und zeigt in einer Auswahl von 49 Hotels auf der ganzen Welt die Besten der vergangenen Jahre sowie topaktuelle Neuentdeckungen. Die eindrucksvollen Bilder, die im Folgenden präsentiert werden, ermöglichen dem Leser, die innovativsten Hotels dieser Welt zu besuchen, zeigen dem Reisenden die unvergleichliche Vielfalt von Stilen und Orten und dienen gleichzeitig Hausbesitzern wie Designern als Inspirationsquelle.

Au cours des dernières années, les hôteliers du monde entier ont adopté des solutions toujours plus audacieuses afin de satisfaire les demandes de commodité, de luxe et de raffinement manifestées par ses clients. Les nouvelles tendances du design créent des espaces qui offrent au visiteur bien plus qu'un lieu d'hébergement, brouillant ainsi la frontière entre le logement, le style de vie et les atmosphères théâtrales. Les hôtels, qui peuvent être de construction récente comme édifiés sur d'anciennes demeures aristocratiques, voire à partir de vieilles usines dont l'esthétique industrielle est préservée grâce au processus de restauration, offrent non seulement leur hospitalité mais également toute une palette de sensations et d'expériences qui couvrent les diverses attentes des voyageurs : de ceux en quête d'un espace similaire à un loft, tout en demeurant à la fois élégant et informel, à ceux recherchant l'ambiance du luxe propre au XIXème siècle. Les hôtels spéciaux, créés en fonction des caractéristiques du climat et de l'endroit parmi lesquelles l'on rencontre, notamment, ceux accueillant les skieurs, ceux constitués de bungalows de style tropical voire les refuges de montagnes plantés dans des recoins isolés, peuvent se faire aussi avant-gardistes que les célèbres hôtels de design s'invitant dans les principales capitales mondiales.

Les hôtels présentés par cet ouvrage sont l'œuvre de professionnels de prestige international – architectes, créateurs et spécialistes divers – qui ont choisi de porter spécialement l'accent sur les détails, recherchant l'originalité dans chacun des aspects considérés. Souvent, les chambres ont été pensées individuellement et selon un thème spécifique, alors que les programmes de l'hôtel ont incorporé des éléments novateurs parmi lesquels l'on relève les jacuzzis, cachés sur des terrasses privées, les salles de jeu, les cours de cuisine, les bibliothèques et les guides personnels. Autre particularisme distinguant ces hôtels : la constante rénovation de leur aspect, toujours surprenant,

qui change au fil des diverses expositions d'œuvres d'art, avec l'évolution des intérieurs et l'apparition de nouveaux services.

Actuellement, les hôtels les plus singuliers se mettent en valeur de par leur capacité à créer des ambiances uniques qui stimulent l'imagination tout en provoquant des sensations mémorables, qu'il s'agisse de nous projeter dans le futur comme pour un retour vers le passé, ou l'entrée dans une nouvelle dimension complètement différente. Nombreux sont ceux qui voient dans ces hôtels l'appartement parfait, qu'il soit citadin ou campagnard, où s'harmonisent l'atmosphère du foyer et l'exceptionnel. Cette harmonie est matérialisée, essentiellement, par la qualité des services offerts, quant au traitement que reçoivent les invités et certains détails qui font de leur visite une expérience merveilleuse échappant aux principes de la normalité.

Cette seconde édition de Cool Hotels, dont la première publication vit le jour en 2001, propose un instantané actualisé des dernières tendances du design hôtelier et passe en revue un répertoire de quarante-neuf hôtels de par le monde, parmi lesquels les meilleurs de l'an passé et les révélations d'aujourd'hui. Les images captivantes présentées à la suite permettent au lecteur de visiter les hôtels les plus marquants du monde dont les différents styles, toujours uniques, et sites saisissants séduiront le voyageur sachant en apprécier le caractère exquis et pourront servir de source d'inspiration tant pour les propriétaires désireux d'introduire quelques changements dans leur demeure que pour les professionnels du secteur.

Durante los últimos años, los hoteleros del mundo entero han adoptado soluciones cada vez más osadas a fin de satisfacer las demandas de comodidad, lujo y exquisitez manifestadas por sus clientes. Las nuevas tendencias del diseño crean espacios que ofrecen al visitante mucho más que un sitio en el que alojarse, difuminando así la frontera entre el hospedaje, el estilo de vida y los ambientes teatrales. Los hoteles, que tanto pueden ser de construcción reciente como edificados a partir de antiguas villas aristocráticas, o incluso a partir de viejas fábricas cuya estética industrial se conserva mediante el proceso de restauración, ofrecen no sólo alojamiento, sino también toda una gama de sensaciones y experiencias que abarca las variadas inquietudes de los viajeros: desde aquéllos que buscan un espacio que se asemeje a un loft, a un mismo tiempo elegante e informal, hasta los que buscan un ambiente de lujo propio del siglo XIX. Los hoteles especiales, creados en función de las características del clima y del lugar en el que se ubican, entre ellos, los que alojan a esquiadores, los que consisten en bungalows de estilo tropical, o los que constituyen refugios de montañas situados en lugares aislados, llegan a ser tan vanguardistas como los famosos hoteles de diseño que se encuentran en las principales capitales del mundo.

Los hoteles que presenta este libro involucran la labor de profesionales de prestigio internacional –arquitectos, diseñadores y diversos especialistas–, quienes han centrado especialmente su atención en los detalles, buscando la originalidad en cada uno de los aspectos considerados. A menudo, las habitaciones han sido diseñadas de forma individual y de acuerdo con un tema específico, mientras que los programas del hotel han incorporado elementos innovadores, entre los que destacan los jacuzzis, ubicados en terrazas privadas, las salas de juego, las clases de cocina, las bibliotecas y los guías personales. Otra peculiaridad que distingue estos hoteles es la constante reno-

vación de su aspecto, siempre sorprendente, que cambia con el paso de las diversas exposiciones de obras de arte, con la modificación de los interiores, y con el surgimiento de nuevos servicios.

Actualmente, los hoteles más asombrosos destacan por su capacidad para crear ambientes únicos que estimulan la imaginación y provocan sensaciones memorables, tanto si se trata de introducirnos en el futuro como de retornar al pasado o de entrar en una dimensión por completo diferente. Son muchas las personas que ven en estos hoteles el apartamento perfecto, ya sea en la ciudad o en el campo, donde armonizan la atmósfera hogareña y la excepcional. A esta conjunción se llega, fundamentalmente, por medio de la calidad de los servicios brindados, en lo que respecta al trato que recibe el huésped y a ciertos detalles que hacen de su visita una experiencia maravillosa, que escapa a los parámetros habituales.

Esta segunda edición de Cool Hotels, cuya primera publicación salió a la luz en el año 2001, ofrece un recuento actualizado de las últimas tendencias del diseño hotelero y pasa revista a un repertorio de cuarenta y nueve hoteles del mundo, entre los que se encuentran los mejores del año pasado y las revelaciones del presente año. Las impactantes imágenes que se presentan a continuación permitirán al lector visitar los hoteles más vanguardistas del mundo, cuyos diferentes estilos, siempre únicos, e impactantes emplazamientos serán del agrado de todo viajero que aprecie la exquisitez y, al mismo tiempo, servirán como fuente de inspiración tanto para los propietarios deseosos de introducir cambios en sus viviendas como para los profesionales del sector.

Nel corso degli ultimi anni, gli albergatori di tutto il mondo hanno adottato soluzioni sempre più audaci al fine di soddisfare le richieste di comfort, lusso e squisitezza manifestate dai loro clienti. Le nuove tendenze del design creano spazi che offrono al visitatore molto più di un semplice luogo dove pernottare, attenuando così i limiti tra l'alloggio, lo stile di vita e gli ambienti teatrali. Gli alberghi, che possono essere sia di costruzione recente che ricavati all'interno di antiche ville aristocratiche, o persino a partire da vecchie fabbriche la cui estetica industriale viene mantenuta mediante un accurato processo di restauro, offrono non solo un alloggio, ma anche una serie di sensazioni ed esperienze che tengono conto delle esigenze e preferenze dei vari tipi di ospiti: da quelli alla ricerca di uno spazio che somigli a un loft, elegante ma allo stesso tempo informale, a quelli che prediligono un ambiente di lusso, proprio del XIX secolo. Le strutture ricettive specializzate, create in base alle caratteristiche del clima e del luogo in cui sono situate – tra queste quelle delle stazioni sciistiche, quelle che consistono in bungalow di stile tropicale, o i rifugi di montagna siti in luoghi isolati – possono essere tanto all'avanguardia come i più famosi hotel attuali dal design più moderno, che si trovano nelle principali capitali del mondo.

Gli alberghi presentati in questo libro includono il lavoro di professionisti di prestigio internazionale – architetti, designer e specialisti vari –, i quali hanno focalizzato la loro attenzione sui dettagli, perseguendo l'originalità in ognuno degli aspetti considerati. Spesso le camere sono state disegnate singolarmente o sono a tema, realizzate d'accordo a un soggetto specifico. Dal canto loro i programmi degli alberghi hanno incluso una serie di elementi e servizi innovativi, tra cui spiccano le vasche idromassaggio, situate in terrazzi privati, le sale da gioco, le lezioni di cucina, le biblioteche e le guide personali. Un'altra peculiarità che distingue questi alberghi è il costante rinnovo del loro aspetto,

sempre sorprendente, che cambia d'accordo con le diverse mostre di opere d'arte, con la modifica degli interni, con il sorgere di nuovi servizi.

Attualmente, gli alberghi più sorprendenti si fanno notare per la loro capacità di creare ambienti unici che stimolano l'immaginazione e suscitano sensazioni memorabili, trasportandoci in epoche passate, catapultandoci verso il futuro o coinvolgendoci in una dimensione completamente nuova. Sono molte le persone che vedono in questi alberghi l'appartamento perfetto, sia in città che in campagna, che abbina con armonia un'atmosfera sia familiare che eccezionale. Questa combinazione ideale si ottiene, principalmente, mediante la qualità dei servizi offerti, la cortesia e disponibilità del personale nei confronti degli ospiti, ed alcuni particolari che rendono il soggiorno un'esperienza meravigliosa, fuori dai parametri convenzionali.

Questa seconda edizione di Cool Hotels, la cui prima pubblicazione vide la luce nel 2001, offre una panoramica aggiornata delle ultime tendenze in fatto di design alberghiero e passa in rassegna un repertorio di quarantanove hotel sparsi per il mondo, che annovera i migliori dell'anno scorso e le rivelazioni di quello presente. Le sbalorditive immagini che si presentano qui di seguito permetteranno al lettore di visitare gli alberghi più all'avanguardia del mondo. I loro stili diversi ed unici, le loro eccellenti ubicazioni saranno graditi da tutti quei viaggiatori che amano la squisitezza e al contempo serviranno da fonte di ispirazione sia per i proprietari desiderosi di apportare modifiche alle loro abitazioni che per i professionisti del settore.

Europe

Austria	Italy
Cyprus	Slovenia
France	Spain
Germany	Switzerland
Greece	UK
Iceland	

Slovenia –
Nebesa

Iceland–
Radisson SAS 1919 Hotel

Germany –
East Hotel
InterContinental Düsseldorf
Radisson SAS Hotel

France –
Hotel Le A
Murano Urban Resort

UK –
Blanch House
The Mandeville Hotel

Spain –
Barcelona Forum AC Hotel
Grand Hotel Central
Hotel Casa Fuster
Hotel RA Beach Thalasso-Spa
Hotel Vincci Condal Mar
La Florida
Palacio del Retiro AC Hotel
Puro

Italy–
Byblos Art Hotel Villa Amistà
Ca Maria Adele
Straf Hotel

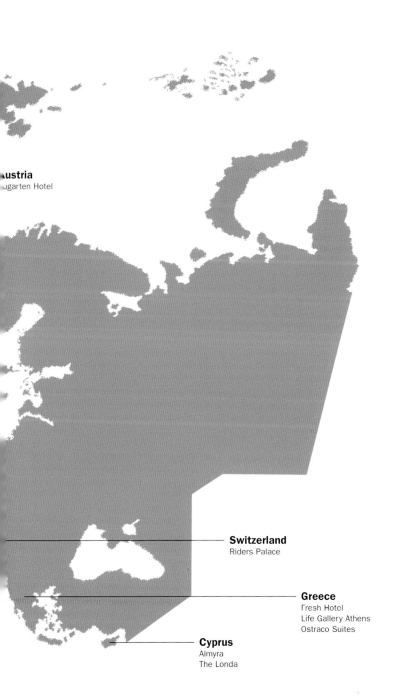

Austria
ugarten Hotel

Switzerland
Riders Palace

Greece
Fresh Hotel
Life Gallery Athens
Ostraco Suites

Cyprus
Almyra
The Londa

Augarten Hotel

Address: Schönaugasse 53, A-8010 Graz, Austria
Tel.: +43 316 208 00
Fax: +43 316 208 0080
www.augartenhotel.at

Architect: Günther Domenig
Opening date: 2000
Photos: Augarten Hotel

19

Style: modern

Rooms: 56

Special features: indoor pool, sun terrace, sauna, solarium, rooftop terrace

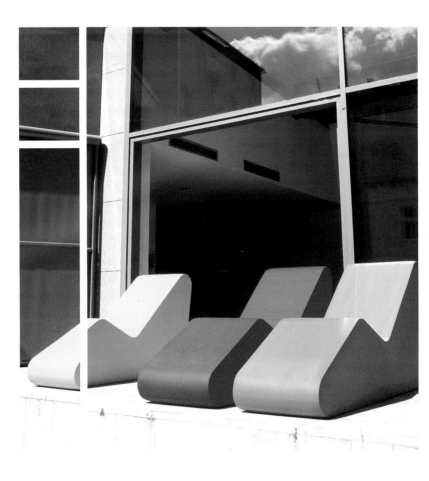

Almyra

Address: PO Box 60136, 8125 Pafos, Cyprus
Tel.: +357 26 933 091
Fax: +357 26 942 818
www.thanoshotels.com

Architect: Joelle Pleot, Tristan Auer
Opening date: 2004
Photos: Giulio Oriani/Vega

27

Style: contemporary seaside

Rooms: 190

Special features: freshwater pools, rooftop terrace, tennis court, children's club

The Londa

Address: 72 George A Street, Potamos Yermasoyias, Yermasoyia
4048 Limassol, Cyprus
Tel.: +357 25 865 555
Fax: +357 25 320 040
www.londahotel.com

Architect: Caruzzo Rancati
Opening date: 2005
Photos: The Londa

Style: contemporary classic

Rooms: 68

Special features: stunning sea-views, spa, pool bar

Hotel Le A

Address: 4, rue d'Artois, 75008 Paris, France
Tel.: +33 1 42 56 99 99
Fax: +33 1 42 56 99 90
www.paris-hotel-a.com

Designer: Frédéric Méchiche
Opening date: 2003
Photos: Hotel Le A

41

Style: contemporary

Rooms: 25

Special features: townhouse feel, bar, art & design library

Murano Urban Resort

Address: 13, boulevard du Temple, 75003 Paris, France
Tel.: +33 1 42 71 20 00
Fax: +33 1 42 71 21 01
www.muranoresort.com

Designers: Christine Derory, Raymond Morel
Opening date: 2005
Photos: Murano Urban Resort

Style: contemporary

Rooms: 52

Special features: color light variator, pool, piano bar

East Hotel

Address: Simon-von-Utrecht-Straße 31, 20359 Hamburg, Germany
Tel.: +49 40 309 930
Fax: +49 40 309 932 00
www.east-hamburg.de

Architects: Jordan Mozer & Associates
Opening date: 2004
Photos: Doug Snower

57

Style: contemporary fusion

Rooms: 103

Special features: sauna, spa, gym, rooftop terrace, virtual putting green

InterContinental Düsseldorf

Address: Königsallee 59, 40215 Düsseldorf, Germany
Tel.: +49 211 8285 0
Fax: +49 211 8285 1111
www.ichotelsgroup.com

Architect: HPP – Hentrich-Petschnigg & Partner
HBA – Hirsch Bedner Associates
Execution: Tombusch & Brumann GmbH (interior)
Opening date: 2005
Photos: Olaf Schiemann

63

Style: modern luxury

Rooms: 286 guest rooms and 32 suites

Special features: ideal location on the main shopping boulevard of Düsseldorf, surprising art concept, largest ballroom in the city

Radisson SAS Hotel

Address: Karl-Liebknecht-Straße 3, 10178 Berlin, Germany
Tel.: +49 30 238 280
Fax: +49 30 238 2810
www.radisson.com

Architect: nps tchoban voss Architekten
Opening date: 2004
Photos: Radisson SAS Hotel, Berlin

Style: contemporary

Rooms: 427

Special features: aquarium with 2,500 tropical fish, indoor pool, sauna

Fresh Hotel

Address: 26 Sophocleus St., 10552 Athens, Greece
Tel.: +30 210 524 8511
Fax: +30 210 524 8517
www.freshhotel.gr

Architect: Zeppos-Georgiadi+Associates
Opening date: 2004
Photos: Fresh Hotel

79

Style: minimalist

Rooms: 133
Special features: steam bath, rooftop terrace, pool

Life Gallery Athens

Address: 103 Thisseos Avenue, 14565 Ekali, Athens, Greece
Tel.: +30 210 626 0400
Fax: +30 210 622 9353
www.lux-hotels.com/gr/life-gallery

Architect: Kline Haller & Vassillis Rodatos Architects
Opening date: 2004
Photos: Life Gallery Athens

Style: minimalist

Rooms: 30

Special features: library specialized in Greek literature and ancient mythology, spa

Ostraco Suites

Address: Drafaki, 846 00 Mykonos, Greece
Tel.: +30 228 902 3396
Fax: +30 228 902 7123
www.ostraco.gr

Architect: Nikos Pitsos & Dimitris Mantikas
Designer: Angelos Angelopoulos
Opening date: 2004
Photos: Ostraco Suites

93

Style: contemporary Mediterranean

Rooms: 24

Special features: individually styled rooms, pool bar, BBQ, boat and plane excursions

Radisson SAS 1919 Hotel

Address: Posthusstraeti 2, Reykjavik 101, Iceland
Tel.: +354 599 1000
Fax: +354 599 1001
www.1919.reykjavik.radissonsas.com

Architect: Björn Guobrandsson
Opening date: 2005
Photos: Radisson SAS 1919 Hotel

101

Style: contemporary rustic

Rooms: 70
Special features: bar, lounge, fitness room

Byblos Art Hotel Villa Amistà

Address: Via Cedrare 78, 37029 Corrubbio di Negarine, Verona, Italy
Tel.: +39 045 6855555
Fax: +39 045 6855500
www.byblosarthotel.com

Designer: Alessandro Mendini
Opening date: 2005
Photos: Ellia Ascheri, Henri del Olmo

107

Style: neo-baroque

Rooms: 70

Special features: 15th century villa, vast collection of designer furnishings and contemporary artworks, individually styled rooms

Ca Maria Adele

Address: Dorsoduro 111, 30123 Venice, Italy
Tel.: +39 041 5203078
Fax: +39 041 5289013
www.camariaadele.it

Designers: Alessio & Nicola Campa
Opening date: 2004
Photos: Ca Maria Adele

117

Style: luxurious eclectic

Rooms: 14

Special features: theme rooms with waterfall showers, lounge
living room

Straf Hotel

Address: Via San Raffaele 3, 20121, Milan, Italy
Tel.: +39 02 805081
Fax: +39 02 89095294
www.straf.it

Architect: Vincenzo de Cotiis
Opening date: 2003
Photos: Yael Pincus

Style: contemporary classic

Rooms: 64

Special features: stunning sea-views, spa, pool bar

Nebesa

Address: Livek 39, 5222 Kobarid, Slovenia
Tel.: +38 653 844 620
www.nebesa.si

Architect: REAL Engineering d.o.o.
Opening date: 2004
Photos: Nebesa

129

Style: contemporary mountain retreat

Rooms: 4 houses

Special features: individual houses with living room and terrace, Hunter Lodge, sauna

Barcelona Forum AC Hotel

Address: Paseo Taulat 278, 08019 Barcelona, Spain
Tel.: +34 934 898 200
Fax: +34 934 898 201
www.ac-hotels.com

Architect: Josep Lluís Mateo & Josep Juanpere
Opening date: 2004
Photos: Gogortza & Llorella

Style: contemporary

Rooms: 368
Special features: Turkish bath, massage room, spa

NATURA CAFE
TERRAZA
PISCINA
▶

Grand Hotel Central

Via Laietana 30, 08003 Barcelona, Spain
Tel.: +34 932 957 900
Fax: +34 932 681 215
www.grandhotelcentral.com

Architect: Oriol Tintoré (renovation)
Designer: Sandra Tarruella and Isabel López
Opening date: 2005
Photos: Grand Hotel Central

Style: classic contemporary

Rooms: 147

Special features: rooftop pool and view over Barcelona, architecture library, original 1920s structure

Hotel Casa Fuster

Address: Paseo de Gracia 132, 08008 Barcelona, Spain
Tel.: +34 932 553 000
Fax: +34 932 553 002
www.hotelescenter.es

Architect: GCA Arquitectos
Opening date: 2004
Photos: Gogortza & Llorella

153

Style: modern eclectic

Rooms: 96

Special features: terrace with panoramic views, solarium, Jacuzzi

Hotel RA Beach Thalasso-Spa

Address: Avenida Sanatori 1, 43880 El Vendrell, Tarragona, Spain
Tel.: +34 977 694 200
Fax: +34 977 692 999
www.epoquehotels.com

Architect: Miquel Espinet & Antonio Ubach
Opening date: 2004
Photos: Pep Escoda

Style: minimalist

Rooms: 143

Special features: piano bar, grill room, terrace bar, thalasso spa

Hotel Vincci Condal Mar

Address: c/ Cristóbal de Moura 160, 08019 Barcelona, Spain
Tel.: +34 914 902 650
Fax: +34 916 626 575
www.vinccihoteles.com

Architect: GCA Arquitectos
Opening date: 2005
Photos: Gogortza & Llorella

Style: contemporary

Rooms: 178

Special features: meeting rooms, international and Mediterranean specialized buffet, exclusive Asian cuisine, swimming-pool, gym

La Florida

Address: Carretera de Vallvidrera al Tibidabo 83–93, 08035 Barcelona, Spain
Tel.: +34 932 593 000
Fax: +34 932 593 001
www.hotellaflorida.com

Architect: Ramón Raventós
Opening date: 2003
Photos: Gogortza & Llorella

Style: urban contemporary

Rooms: 74

Special features: historical context and architectural
features, rooftop terrace and views,
hydrotherapy

Palacio del Retiro AC Hotel

Address: Alfonso XII 14, 28014 Madrid, Spain
Tel.: +34 915 237 460
Fax: +34 915 237 461
www.ac-hoteles.com

Architect: José Luis Oriol y Uriguen
Opening date: 2004
Photos: Jordi Miralles

193

Style: classical modern

Rooms: 51

Special features: 19th century building, artworks, Turkish bath

Puro

Address: Monte Negro 12, 07012 Palma de Mallorca, Spain
Tel.: +34 971 425 450
Fax: +34 971 425 451
www.purohotel.com

Architect: Alvaro Planchuelo
Opening date: 2004
Photos: Hotel Puro

Style: exotic contemporary

Rooms: 26

Special features: spa, two swimming pools, poolside cabanas, tennis courts

Riders Palace

Address: 7032 Laax, Switzerland
Tel.: +41 81 927 97 00
www.riderspalace.ch

Architect: René Meierhofer
Opening date: 2001
Photos: courtesy Laax

Style: modern high-tech

Rooms: 70

Special features: glass façade, multimedia rooms, live concerts

Blanch House

Address: 17 Atlingworth Street, Brighton BN2 1PL, UK
Tel.: +44 127 360 3504
Fax: +44 127 368 9813
www.blanchhouse.co.uk

Architect: Amanda Blanch
Opening date: 2000
Photos: Leigh Simpson

217

Style: contemporary

Rooms: 178

Special features: 12-floor atrium, rooftop solarium, open-air bar

The Mandeville Hotel

Address: Mandeville Place, London W1U 2BE, UK
Tel.: +44 207 935 5599
Fax: +44 207 935 9588
www.mandeville.co.uk

Designer: Stephen Ryan
Opening date: 2005
Photos: James Balston

225

Style: Modern regency

Rooms: 142

Special features: Flat-screen interactive LCD screens, power shower, penthouse suite

Americas

Argentina

Canada

Mexico

USA

Mexico —————
Básico

Argentina —————
otel & Universe

Faena Hotel & Universe

Address: Martha Salotti 445, Puerto Madero Este
C1107CMB Buenos Aires, Argentina
Tel.: +54 11 4010 9000
Fax: +54 11 4010 9001
www.faenahotelanduniverse.com

Designer: Philippe Starck
Opening date: 2004
Photos: Nikolas Koenig

233

Style: modern romantic

Rooms: 83

Special features: boutique, library lounge, hammam

Drake Hotel

Address: 1150 Queen Street West, M6J 1J3 Toronto, Ontario, Canada
Tel.: +1 416 531 5042
Fax: +1 416 531 9493
www.thedrakehotel.ca

Architect: Paul Syme Architect
Opening date: 2004
Photos: George Whiteside/Stipco photographics

241

Style: contemporary

Rooms: 19

Special features: corner café, dining rooms, underground entertainment venue, sky yard patio, yoga and spa treatment room

Opus Hotel

Address: 322 Davie Street, Vancouver, British Columbia V6B 5Z6, Canada
Tel.: +1 604 642 6787
Fax: +1 604 642 6780
www.opushotel.com

Architect: Paul Merrick Architects
Design: Architectura Planning Architecture Interiors
Opening date: 2002
Photos: Rob Melnychuk

249

Style: contemporary hip

Rooms: 97

Special features: personalized rooms, heated bathroom floors, l'Occitane bath products, oxygen "shots"

Básico

Address: Playa del Carmen, 77710 Quintana Roo, Mexico
Tel.: +52 984 879 4448
Fax: +52 984 879 4449
www.hotelbasico.com

Architects: Moisés Isón, José Antonio Sánchez/Central de Arquitectura
Designer: Héctor Galván/Omelette
Opening date: 2005
Photos: Undine Pröhl

Style: tropical chic

Rooms: 15

Special features: seafood specialty restaurant, rooftop terrace and pool, Juice Stand, dance lessons

Hotel Gansevoort

Address: 18 9th Avenue (at 13th Street), New York, NY 10014, USA
Tel.: +1 212 206 6700
Fax: +1 212 255 5858
www.hotelgansevoort.com

Architect: The Stephen B. Jacobs Group, PC
Opening date: 2004
Photos: David Joseph

263

Style: contemporary hip

Rooms: 187

Special features: G Spa & Lounge, 45-foot heating outdoor glass-surrounded pool with underwater music, event loft

Maritime Hotel

Address: 363 West 16th Street, New York, NY 10011, USA
Tel.: +1 212 242 4300
Fax: +1 212 242 1188
www.themaritimehotel.com

Architect: Eric Goode and Sean MacPherson
Opening date: 2003
Photos: Gogortza & Llorella

269

Style: modern elegance

Rooms: 125

Special features: five-foot wide porthole windows, Japanese restaurant, 10,000 square-foot garden

On Rivington

Address: 107 Rivington Street, New York, NY 10002, USA
Tel.: +1 212 475 2600
Fax: +1 212 475 5959
www.hotelonrivington.com

Architect: GrzywinskiPons Architects
Opening date: 2005
Photos: Floto + Warner

Style: classic contemporary

Rooms: 110

Special features: in-room spas, library, 21-foot-high glass atrium dining room

The Dorset Hotel

Address: 1720 Collins Avenue, Miami Beach, FL 33139, USA
Tel.: +1 305 938 6000
Fax: +1 305 938 6001
www.dorsethotelmiamibeach.com

Architect: Günter Domenig
Opening date: 2004
Photos: Pep Escoda

285

Style: contemporary art deco

Rooms: 52

Special features: H_2O bath products, rooftop pool, solarium

The Parker Palm Springs

Address: 4200 East Palm Canyon Drive, Palm Springs, CA 92264, USA
Tel.: +1 760 770 5000
Fax: +1 760 324 2188
www.theparkerpalmsprings.com

Architect: Jonathan Adler
Opening date: 2004
Photos: Nikolas Koenig

295

Style: bohemian retro chic

Rooms: 144, 1 two-bedroom house, and 12 villas

Special features: yacht club spa, 10,000 square foot banquet facility

The Setai

Address: 2001 Collins Avenue, Miami Beach, FL 33139, USA
Tel.: +1 305 520 6000
Fax: +1 305 520 6600
www.setai.com

Architect: Jean Michel Gathy and Denniston International
Opening date: 2004
Photos: The Setai

303

Style: contemporary Asian

Rooms: 125

Special features: in-room "rainfall" showers, beach bar, three pools

Thunderbird Hotel

Address: 601 West San Antonio, Marfa, TX 79843, USA
Tel.: +1 432 729 1984
Fax: +1 432 729 1989
www.thunderbirdmarfa.com

Architect: Bob Harris of Lake/Flato Architects
Designer: R. L. Fletcher, Jamey Garza, Liz Lambert
Opening date: 2005
Photos: Clayton Maxwell

311

Style: country modern

Rooms: 40

Special features: heated swimming pool, vinyl library, record players, vintage typewriters and polaroid cameras to borrow, luxurious bath products

Asia, Africa, Oceania

China

Japan

Morocco

New Zealand

Oman

Singapore

South Africa

South Korea

Turkey

Turkey
Hillside Su

Morocco
Dar Les Cigognes

South Africa
Singita
The Grand Café and Rooms
The Outpost

Oman
The Chedi Muscat

China
Hotel Kassel Grimm

Singapore
The Scarlet

Japan
Conrad Tokyo

South Korea
W Seoul Walkerhill

New Zealand
The Spire Queenstown

Hotel Kassel Grimm

Address: No.1 Nan-An-De Rd., An-Ting New Town Jia Ding District
Shanghai, China
Tel.: +86 2 161 231 919

Architect: MoHen Design International
Opening date: 2005
Photos: Maoder Chou

319

Style: high-tech

Rooms: 16

Special features: specialty hotel served for the F1 car racing players, LED lighting, high-tech multimedia

Conrad Tokyo

1-9-1 Higashi-Shinbashi, Minato-ku, Tokyo 105-7337, Japan
Tel.: +81 3 6388 8000
Fax: +81 3 6388 8001
www.conradtokyo.co.jp

Architect: Takenaka Corporation, GA Design London
Opening date: 2005
Photos: Conrad Tokyo

325

Style: Japanese modern luxury

Rooms: 290

Special features: minimum 515 square foot rooms with
37-inch plasma TV, satellite channels
and wireless phone

Dar Les Cigognes

Address: 108, rue de Berima Medina, 40000 Marrakech, Morocco
Tel.: +212 24 38 27 40
Fax: +212 24 38 47 67

www.lescigognes.com

Architect: Charles Boccara
Opening date: 2004
Photos: Dar Les Cigognes

333

Style: Moroccan luxury

Rooms: 11

Special features: 17th century structure, in-room fireplaces, central courtyards

The Spire Queenstown

Address: Church Lane, PO Box 1129, 9197 Queenstown, New Zealand
Tel.: +64 3 441 0004
Fax: +64 3 441 0003
www.thespirehotels.com

Designer: Stewart Harris/Martin Hughes Interior Architecture
Opening date: 2005
Photos: The Spire

339

Style: contemporary cool

Rooms: 10

Special features: interactive multimedia system, Wi-Fi network, 42-inch plasma TV, large covered balcony

The Chedi Muscat

Address: North Ghubra 232, Way 3215, Street 46, 133 Muscat, Oman
Tel.: +968 24 52 44 00
Fax: +968 24 49 34 85
www.ghmhotels.com

Architect: Jean Michel Gathy and Denniston International
Opening date: 2002
Photos: The Chedi Muscat

345

Style: traditional Omani

Rooms: 151

Special features: Mediterranean and Asian restaurant, spa, two swimming pools, poolside cabanas, tennis courts

The Scarlet

Address: 33 Erskine Road, Singapore 069333
Tel.: +65 6511 3333
Fax: +65 6511 3303
www.thescarlethotel.com

Architect: Hia HK
Opening date: 2004
Photos: The Scarlet

355

Style: classical hip

Rooms: 84

Special features: theme rooms, pool terrace, spa

Singita

Address: PO Box 23367, Claremont 7735, Cape Town, South Africa
Tel.: +27 216 833 424
Fax: +27 216 833 502
www.singita.com

Architects: Andrew Makin, Joy Brasler/Omm Design Workshop
Opening date: 2003
Photos: Singita Lebombo

Style: contemporary mountain retreat

Rooms: 15

Special features: guided bush walks, library, wine cellar, health spa

The Grand Café and Rooms

Address: 27 Main Road, Plettenberg Bay, 6600 Cape Town, South Africa
Tel.: +27 445 333 301
Fax: +27 445 333 301
www.thegrand.co.za

Designer: Gail Behr
Opening date: 2004
Photos: Jac de Villiers

371

Style: modern romantic
Rooms: 5

Special features: café, oversized king beds, double showers, room access to pool deck

The Outpost

Address: 10 Bompas Road, Dunkeld West, 2146 Johannesburg
　　　　　South Africa
Tel.: +27 11 341 0282
Fax: +27 11 341 0281
www.theoutpost.co.za

Architect: Enrico Daffonchio
Opening date: 2003
Photos: Giulio Oriani/Vega

379

Style: contemporary rustic

Rooms: 12

Special features: pool deck, visits to Crooks Corner, Thulamela, Makuleke village and Kruger National Park

W Seoul Walkerhill

Address: 21 Kwangjang Dong - A, Kwangjin Gu, Seoul 143708, South Korea
Tel.: +82 2 465 2222
Fax: +82 2 450 4989
www.whotels.com/seoul

Architect: Ilan Waisbrod/Studio Gaia
Designer: Studio Gaia
Opening date: 2004
Photos: W Seoul Walkerhill/Studio Gaia

387

Style: contemporary Asian

Rooms: 253
Special features: boutique, hair salon, indoor pool

Hillside Su

Address: Konyaalti, 07050 Antalya, Turkey
Tel.: +90 242 249 07 00
Fax: +90 242 249 07 07
www.hillside.com.tr

Architect: Eren Talu
Opening date: 2003
Photos: Tamer Yilmaz

395

Style: minimalist

Rooms: 294

Special features: indoor pool, pool bar, Maxi Bar, mood lighting, balcony with sofa

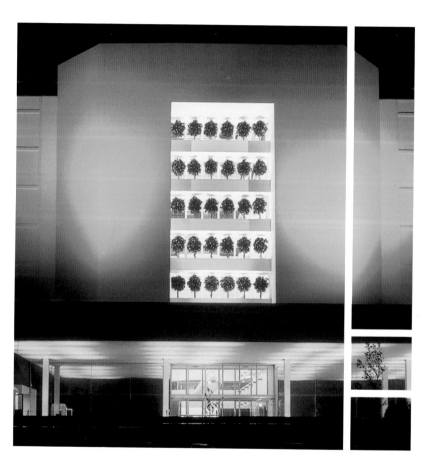

Other Designpocket titles by teNeues

African Interior Design 3-8238-4563-2
Airline Design 3-8327-9055-1
Asian Interior Design 3-8238-4527-6
Bathroom Design 3-8238-4523-3
Beach Hotels 3-8238-4566-7
Berlin Apartments 3-8238-5596-4
Boat Design 3-8327-9054-3
Café & Restaurant Design 3-8327-9017-9
Car Design 3-8238-4561-6
Cool Hotels Cool Prices 3-8327-9134-5
Cool Hotels Africa/Middle East 3-8327-9051-9
Cool Hotels America 3-8238-4565-9
Cool Hotels Asia/Pacific 3-8238-4581-0
Cool Hotels Ecological 3-8327-9135-3
Cool Hotels Europe 3-8238-4582-9
Cool Hotels Romantic Hideaways 3-8327-9136-1
Cosmopolitan Hotels 3-8238-4546-2
Country Hotels 3-8238-5574-3
Food Design 3-8327-9053-5
Furniture Design 3-8238-5575-1
Garden Design 3-8238-4524-1
Italian Interior Design 3-8238-5495-X
Kitchen Design 3-8238-4522-5
London Apartments 3-8238-5558-1
Los Angeles Houses 3-8238-5594-8
Miami Houses 3-8238-4545-4
New Scandinavian Design 3-8327-9052-7
Pool Design 3-8238-4531-4
Product Design 3-8238-5597-2
Rome Houses 3-8238-4564-0
San Francisco Houses 3-8238-4526-8
Shop Design 3-8327-9104-3
Ski Hotels 3-8238-4543-8
Spa & Wellness Hotels 3-8238-5595-6
Sport Design 3-8238-4562-4
Staircase Design 3-8238-5572-7
Sydney Houses 3-8238-4525-X
Tropical Houses 3-8238-4544-6
Wine & Design 3-8327-9137-X

Each volume:
12.5 x 18.5 cm
400 pages
c. 400 color illustrations